FANTASTICALLY
GREAT
WOMEN
WHO CHANGED THE
WORLD

Kate Pankhurst

BLOOMSBURY

LONDON OXFORD NEW YORK NEW DELHI SYDNEY

EMMELINE PANKHURST

VOTES FOR WOMEN

Rosa Parks

Anne Frank

SACAGAWEA

Agent Fifi

How did they become so fantastically amazing and great?!

The women in this book didn't set out to be thought of as 'great'. They achieved extraordinary things simply by following their hearts, talents and dreams. They didn't listen when people said they couldn't do something. They dared to be different. And some of them couldn't resist a crazy adventure, or three.

WHO WROTE THESE WONDERFUL BOOKS?

SENSE and SENSIBILITY 1811
PRIDE and PREJUDICE 1813
Mansfield Park 1814
EMMA 1815
NORTHANGER ABBEY 1817
PERSUASION 1818

Shhhh! When her first book was published, British writer Jane Austen couldn't tell anyone she was the author! In 1811 people thought it wasn't right for a woman to have a job, no matter how talented they were.

The books Jane wrote were SO heartbreaking, romantic and thrilling that they are still enjoyed two hundred years later. They are some of the best stories ever created.

MEET SOME OF JANE'S HEROINES, HEROES AND VILLAINS ...

Jane

Mr Darcy is such a BORE!

A witty heroine who speaks her mind even though a proper 'lady' was not supposed to have an opinion.

Elizabeth Bennet and Mr Darcy
PRIDE and PREJUDICE

Why won't you marry me?!

Dashingly handsome, and wealthy. Changes his snooty ways to win Elizabeth Bennet's heart.

Austen

A vain and nasty upper class man, who thinks being beautiful is more important than being a nice person.

How UGLY!

Sir Walter Elliot PERSUASION

How romantic!

Decides to help her friends and family find the right husband, but discovers she has a lot to learn about life and love.

Emma Woodhouse EMMA

Who does she think she is?

Mrs Norris MANSFIELD PARK

A beastly woman in a bonnet who is really horrible to her niece, Fanny Price, who comes from a poor family.

Catherine Morland NorthanGER ABBEY

GASP!

Struggles to learn that real life doesn't work out like the dramatic novels she loves to read.

In secret letters to her sister, Jane writes of having her own heart broken, just like the heroines she wrote about, by a man called Tom Lefroy. The two weren't allowed to marry because Jane's family was not rich.

With no husband, Jane had to rely on her family for money, until her books became popular!

SHE SWAM HER OWN STROKE!

GERTRUDE EDERLE

ESSENTIAL CHANNEL SWIMMER KIT:

A TWO PIECE SWIM SUIT:
Rather than wear a heavy woollen swimsuit, Trudy made herself one of the first two piece bathing suits from underwear. (Men swam the channel naked!)

GREASE!
Trudy's whole body was smothered in grease to keep her warm in the cold water.

A BRIGHT RED SWIMMING CAP
So onlookers could spot her in the waves.

ENG

In the 1920s, teenage Olympic medal-winning swimming sensation Gertrude Ederle from New York, USA, wanted to prove that a woman could complete a swimming challenge said to be as **DIFFICULT** and **DANGEROUS** as climbing Mount Everest. Gertrude (or Trudy) wanted to be the first woman to swim across the freezing waters of the **ENGLISH CHANNEL**.

People wondered if Gertrude's plan was a length too far, especially as her first attempt in 1925 had failed due to bad weather. But she didn't give up ...

THREE men have swum the Channel. I can too!

GOGGLES
To stop sea water stinging her eyes.

"A GIRL SHOULD BE TWO THINGS: WHO AND WHAT SHE WANTS."

COCO CHANEL

in 1910.

Fashion designer, Gabrielle Chanel, or 'Coco' to her friends, opened her first shop in Paris, France,

At that time, women dressed in a very formal way. Coco didn't think this suited the changing lives of women. It was time for a new approach to fashion. Coco SNIP, SNIP, SNIPPED different parts from clothing, making them into garments suitable for the modern woman – to do whatever she pleased in!

UNCOMFORTABLE CORSETS?

SNIP!
(OH LA LA!)

POINTLESS BOWS AND RIBBONS?

SNIP!

AU REVOIR!

GIANT FANCY FEATHERY HATS?

SNIP!
(SACRE BLEU!)

The results of Coco's SNIP, SNIP, SNIPPING paved the way for how we dress today.

SPORTS WEAR
In 1914 Coco used jersey fabric, previously only ever used to make men's underwear, to make clothes for active women, including this swimming costume!

Coco designed clothes for rich customers, but she came from a poor family and worked hard to build her business.

PYJAMAS
Until Coco launched a range of women's pyjamas in 1918, they were only ever worn by men.

TROUSERS
Yes, trousers! Coco was one of the first women to wear trousers. She included them in her 1930 collection.

Coco caused a stir in 1917 when she cut her hair short!

"Fashion is not something that exists in dresses only. Fashion is in the sky, in the street, fashion has to do with ideas. The way we live, what is happening."

THE LITTLE BLACK DRESS
Before Coco designed this dress in 1926, a black dress wasn't considered fancy enough to look good.

Frida Kahlo

Mexican artist Frida Kahlo's life wasn't always easy, but she turned her experiences into **unique** and **wonderful** works of art.

In 1925, aged eighteen, Frida was training to be a doctor when she was in a serious traffic accident. Her injuries meant that she would never be well enough to finish medical school.

While recovering in hospital, Frida began painting pictures of herself, and her life changed forever. Painting helped Frida to feel better. She decided that she wouldn't waste another moment of life. She would paint it instead!

I was very interested in the ancient people who lived in mexico— the <u>AZTECS</u>. They thought dogs acted as guides, so I painted dogs when I was thinking about making <u>BIG</u> decisions.

ITZCUINTLI DOG WITH ME, 1938

FRIDA'S FEELINGS: Frida laughed a lot but she always painted herself looking very serious. This was because she wanted to find more unusual ways to show what she was feeling, so instead she painted curious images as clues ...

In this painting my hair is tied up with ribbons. I wanted to show how it feels to piece things back together after an argument.

family was very important to me. I painted my pet monkeys very close to me to show this.

Frida loved animals and had LOTS of pets.

SELF PORTRAIT WITH MONKEYS, 1943

SELF PORTRAIT WITH BRAID, 1941

viva la vida!

VIVA LA VIDA, WATERMELONS, 1954

FASCINATING FRIDA: People were very interested in Frida because she used her art to say exactly what she thought. She didn't want to hide anything about herself – something unusual for a woman at the time. This is why Frida exaggerated her eyebrows and facial hair in her paintings. Frida was very proud of being a Mexican woman and always wore colourful traditional clothing, jewellery and elaborate hairstyles.

VIVA LA VIDA! Frida painted over 200 artworks which are now famous all over the world, but over her lifetime her health gradually became worse. Even when she was very ill, Frida still wanted to live life to the full. In her last painting, a still life of watermelons, she wrote the words 'VIVA LA VIDA!'. This means: 'LONG LIVE LIFE!' Frida had a truly unique way of looking at the world. It was this that made her one of the most important artists of all time.

Marie Curie

Questions, questions.
Marie had so many questions about science.

Marie came from a poor family in Poland. She saved and struggled to study science at university in Paris, France – and dedicated her life to finding answers that gave the world treatments for serious illnesses.

It was in Paris that Marie became intrigued by a recent mind-boggling scientific discovery... **X-rays!**

Marie's research wasn't all **fizzing** and **whizzing** and exciting **explosions**. There was lots of watching and waiting until ...

Fascinating! Hmmm I wonder if there are any natural substances that give off radiation?

X-rays were first studied in 1895, by German physicist Wilhelm Röntgen. They are invisible rays that pass through solid objects, like our bodies. X-rays are a type of radiation.

$$\left(\tau^2 d\varphi^2 + d\tau^2\right)\left(\frac{\psi_0}{v} + \psi\right)^2 = v^4 d\varphi$$

WOW! I have discovered two brand new elements* — polonium and radium! Both glow and give off a strange invisible radiation. They are RADIOACTIVE!* Hmmm. I wonder if either of them is useful?

Ra

Po

Further experiments revealed that radium was a **wonder element** — it could be used to treat people with cancer.

In 1903 and 1911 Marie was given the world's top award for science — the Nobel Prize. She is the only woman to have won the prize **twice**.

*Element: The metals, minerals, liquids and gases that the world is made up of. Finding a new one is BIG news!

*RADIOACTIVE: Marie said that substances that gave off radiation were radioactive. (Marie Curie was the first person to use this term.)

84
88

Radium

$E - 1 -$
$\frac{E}{c_0}$

RISKY RADIATION
Marie liked to sleep beside a gently glowing jar of radium but didn't realise this was dangerous! Marie felt ill a lot of the time. We now know she was suffering from radiation poisoning.

She walked in the footsteps of... DINOSAURS!

Mary Anni

Mary's dog TRAY

Imagine what could be beneath our feet!

Mary Anning was born in Lyme Regis, England, 1799. At the time people believed that the world was only thousands of years old. Mary's interest in fossils helped prove that the world is actually millions and millions of years old.

Mary's family made a living by selling fossils they found on the beach to wealthy tourists. In the early 1800s nobody was quite sure what these fossils were. Mary was intrigued and went on to make some **MONSTER** discoveries!

FOSSIL FACT:

Fossils form over millions of years when minerals fill the space in and around skeletons, footprints – and even poo – left behind by creatures that lived long, long ago!

1812: Mary discovers the skeleton of a creature that has never been seen before. Scientists come to see it and name the prehistoric sea monster **ICHTHYOSAUR!**

Mary was very good at fossil hunting. FAR better than the male scientists who wrote books about the fossils she found.

But for years, because she was a poor woman who had never been to school, nobody bothered to mention Mary's hard work.

Today Mary is recognised as one of the first, and most important **paleontologists** (that's a scientist who studies dinosaurs) in history.

HUGE monsters once swam in the sea!

RUFF!

WOW! I'm a paleontologist!

Lots of people wondered what Bezoar Stones were. Mary correctly suggested that they were fossiled dinosaur POO!

1820: Mary finds the skeleton of a FIVE METRE long sea creature! Again, scientists rush to the new discovery. The creature is named **PLESIOSAUR.**

1828: Mary uncovers the skeleton of a **PTEROSAUR** – a flying dinosaur that had never been found in Britain before.

THE WONDERFUL ADVENTURES of Mrs SEACOLE IN MANY LANDS...

JUST TRY TELLING MARY SEACOLE THAT SHE COULDN'T DO SOMETHING. IT WOULD ONLY MAKE HER MORE DETERMINED TO FOLLOW HER HEART.

RUSSIA

We know all about Mary because she wrote this thrilling book about her life!

CRIMEA

BLACK SEA

AEGEAN SEA

Mary made the long journey to the Crimea – a scary, war-torn place – and built her own hospital! (Although she called it a hotel.)

THE BRITISH HOTEL

If they don't want me I'll go to the Crimea anyway. I will build my own hospital!

A half Scottish half Jamaican nurse? I just don't think you know enough about proper medicine.

Welcome! I don't care if you are British or Russian. An injured man is an injured man.

In **1854** Mary decided to travel from her home in Jamaica, all the way to England. She wanted to join a group of nurses going to help soldiers injured in the Crimean War. (Britain, France, Turkey and Sardinia were fighting Russia in the Crimea, part of Russia.)

Mary, who had worked as a nurse in a hospital run by her mother, was desperate to help the British troops. But she didn't get the job.

It didn't take long for Mary to figure out that the men's injuries were not the only things killing them.

The cold and hunger is killing these men. Something must be done!

Who Will Save Mrs Seacole?

When the war ended, in **1856**, Mary returned to Britain a heroine – but without any money at all. She spent everything she had helping soldiers at the British Hotel.

Fortunately, Mary's kindness and hard work was not forgotten by those she had nursed, and by others who heard of her good deeds. Money was donated to ensure that Mary wouldn't ever go cold or hungry.

Mary provided hot food and opened a shop selling fresh fruit and vegetables, and warm clothing.

Lets call her Mother Seacole!

SOUP! These men need soup!

If it wasn't for mary I wouldn't eat for days.

AMELIA EARHART

Adventure-loving American pilot Amelia Earhart wanted to become the first ever woman to fly solo across the vast Atlantic Ocean. Even though the dangerous journey had only been completed solo by one man before, and many others had died attempting it, Amelia was still determined to let her dreams take flight ...

THE ADVENTURE STARTS HERE!

20th May 1932, Amelia takes off from Harbour Grace, Newfoundland, Canada headed for Paris, France.

Only 3200 kilometres to go!

UP! UP! UP!

Aviator ATTIRE!

fur-Lined coat

goggles

cap

flying pants

STORMY SKIES!

Strong winds and icy conditions cause mechanical problems. Amelia realises she isn't going to make it to Paris ...

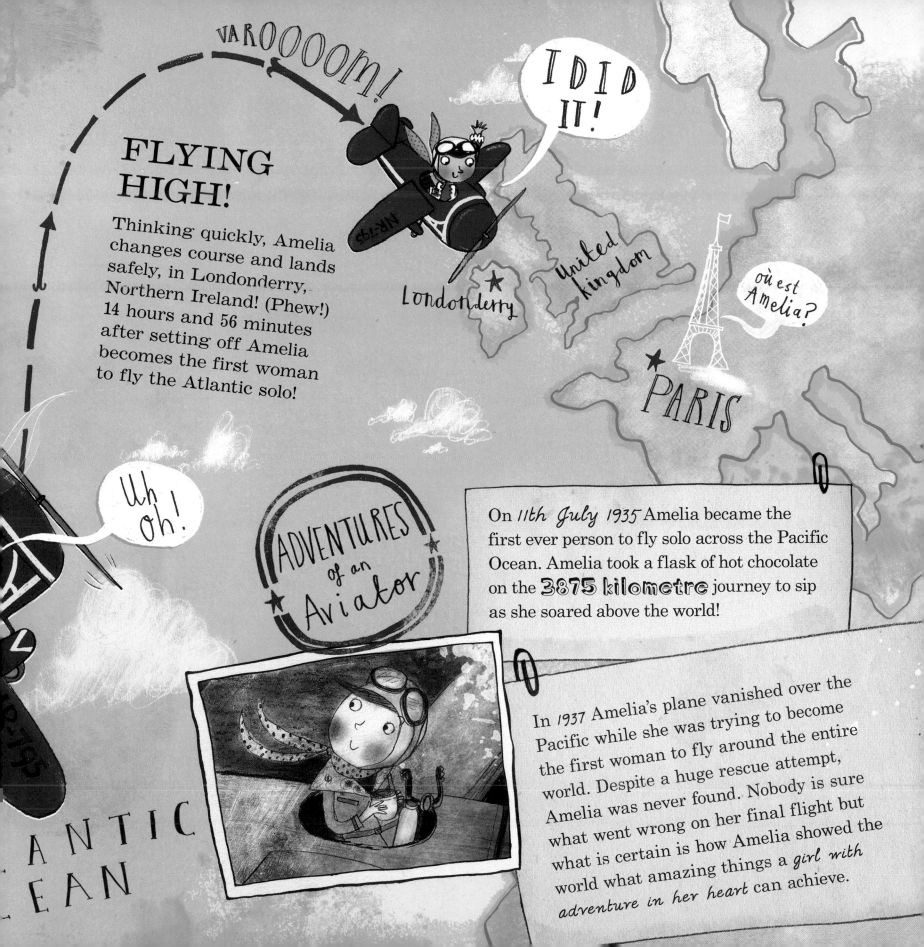

VAROOOOM!

I DID IT!

FLYING HIGH!

Thinking quickly, Amelia changes course and lands safely, in Londonderry, Northern Ireland! (Phew!) 14 hours and 56 minutes after setting off Amelia becomes the first woman to fly the Atlantic solo!

Londonderry

United Kingdom

où est Amelia?

PARIS

Uh Oh!

ADVENTURES of an Aviator

On 11th July 1935 Amelia became the first ever person to fly solo across the Pacific Ocean. Amelia took a flask of hot chocolate on the **3875 kilometre** journey to sip as she soared above the world!

In 1937 Amelia's plane vanished over the Pacific while she was trying to become the first woman to fly around the entire world. Despite a huge rescue attempt, Amelia was never found. Nobody is sure what went wrong on her final flight but what is certain is how Amelia showed the world what amazing things a *girl with adventure in her heart* can achieve.

ATLANTIC OCEAN

Agent Fifi

Tally ho girls! Lets win this war!

REAL NAME:

Marie Christine Chilver

FACTS: During World War Two, in 1940, twenty-year-old Marie was a university student studying languages in Paris, France. Germany invaded and Marie was sent to a prison camp for British women. But Marie hatched a cunning plan and escaped back to Britain. The government was impressed by how daring Marie had been. She was given a secret identity and a very important job to do ...

SECRET MISSION

SEPTEMBER 1942, WORLD WAR TWO

Agent Fifi,

You must test our trainee spies to see if they can keep a secret. If they can be tricked by you – a British Agent – who knows what they might accidentally say to an enemy agent if we let them become proper spies.

We know you can do it Fifi. Everyone says you are a 'woman of outstanding capacity' and you are not just our secret agent. You are 'our special agent'.

Sincerely

SPECIAL OPERATIONS EXECUTIVE,
THE BRITISH INTELLIGENCE SERVICE

FIFI'S SPILL THE BEANS TEST:

Trainee spies had to pass tests in map reading, secret codes, parachuting, explosives and disguises. But Agent Fifi's test was by far the most difficult – Fifi worked undercover so trainees didn't even know they were being tested!

FIFI'S SECRET MISSION TOP TIPS:

TIP ONE: Have a spiffingly convincing cover story.

To make my cover story more convincing I wrote articles for real magazines!

I pretended to be a journalist so that nobody would guess I was actually a secret agent.

TIP TWO: Become jolly good at keeping trainee spies under surveillance, observing their spying techniques.

They have no idea I am watching their every move!

We have top secret work to do!

Fifi received detailed descriptions of the target trainee spy's appearance:

TARGET: Two women, one with dark hair, dark eyes and good teeth. The other is of small build. Hair has auburn tinge and she has a 'pouty' expression.

TIP THREE: Be prepared to travel anywhere at a moment's notice. Targets may be located in cafés, restaurants or even the zoo.

Of course you can trust me!

Target: Dark Hair, bushy eyebrows. Will be at the Giraffe House, London Zoo, 2:30pm.

TIP FOUR: One must have exceedingly sharp conversation skills to convince targets to share top secret information.

Target spilled the beans. They are unsuitable for secret missions.

TIP FIVE: Be frightfully decisive when writing a report about your mission.

Fifi's reports said whether a trainee could be trusted or not. It was very important that only the best trainees became proper spies. If they were to be tricked by a real enemy agent, vital missions could fail and lives might be lost.

TOP SECRET

Keeping secrets from the enemy was so important that Agent Fifi had to promise never to talk about her job, not even to her family. Even after the war was won nobody knew about her remarkable job.

Very recently, after more than 70 years, Fifi's files were made public. It's now no secret what an amazing undercover agent Fifi was.

THE CORPS OF DISCOVERY

In May 1804, explorers Lewis and Clark formed the corps of discovery – a group aiming to map the uncharted west of the USA.

Travelling in the corps, over the vast Rocky Mountains, down rushing river rapids and through raging storms, were over forty men – and one Native American teenage girl, who had just had a baby ...

FOLLOW THE ARROWS TO TRACK THE JOURNEY OF

S A

When Native Americans saw Sacagawea and her baby they trusted that the Corps must have **peaceful intentions**.

GULP! GULP!

We come in peace!

The explorers faced bear attacks and swarms of mosquitoes!

RARR!

PACIFIC OCEAN

I recognise that mountain.

Sacagawea **recognised the landscape** nearby to the Shoshone tribe she grew up in. She was able to show Lewis and Clark the **best route.**

CACAWEA

I travelled the whole journey with my newborn baby on my back.

Considered the property of men in their tribes, life was hard for Native American women. As a child, Sacagawea was kidnapped from the Shoshone tribe she belonged to by the Hidatsa, another tribe who she lived with until Lewis and Clark met her. Sacagawea spoke the languages of both tribes so she was brought on the journey as a translator. It didn't take long for Sacagawea to prove herself useful in lots of other ways ...

Always **calm in a crisis**, Sacagawea rescued vital equipment from being washed away.

Sacagawea travelled over **6400 kilometres** on foot, horseback and by boat!

Liquorice root anyone?

Food was difficult to find on the expedition, but Sacagawea knew how to **forage** for roots and berries.

An Unexpected Ending to the Expedition
The expedition was completed in **1806**. Sacagawea's efforts meant that Lewis and Clark saw her as an equal – something amazing for a woman at that time, especially a Native American woman.

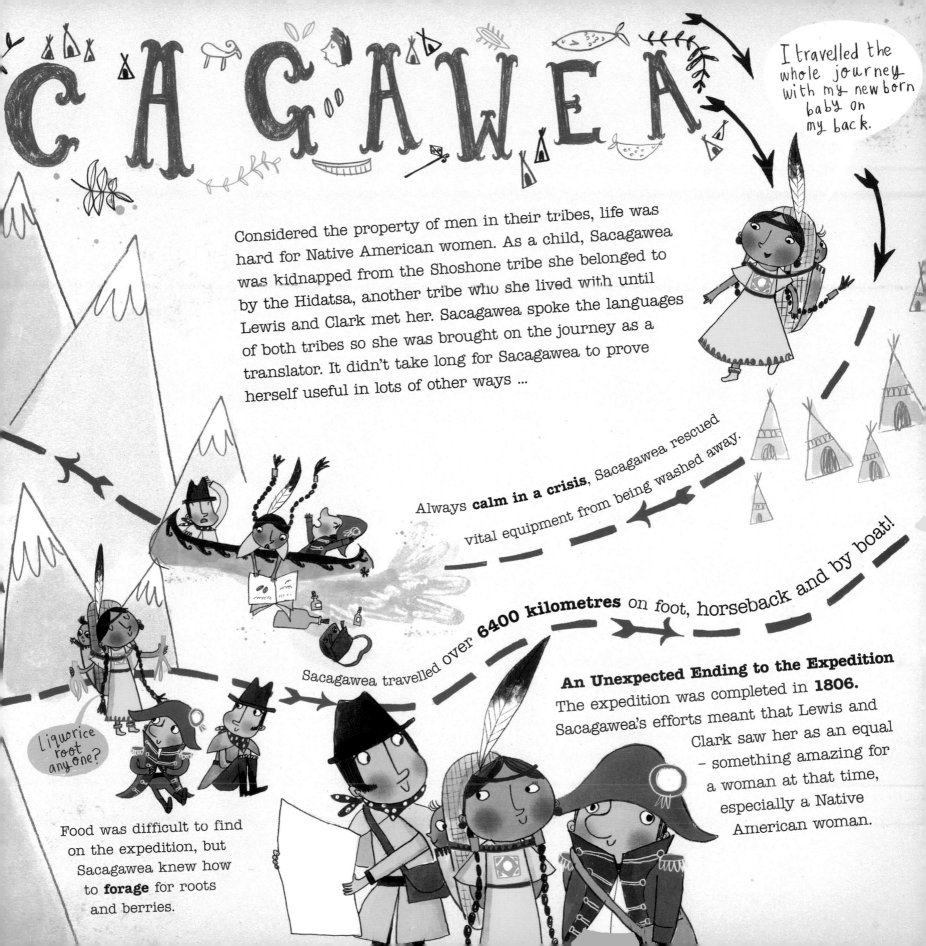

EMMELINE PANKHURST

MOST PASSIONATE AND DETERMINED CAMPAIGNER THAT THERE SHOULD INDEED BE

VOTES FOR WOMEN

I n England, in 1903 Emmeline Pankhurst set out to inspire women from all walks of life – rich and poor, young and old – to campaign for an end to the law that said women weren't allowed to vote. These women became known as the suffragettes.

With Mrs Pankhurst as their leader, the suffragettes were determined to show those people who didn't think women had anything important to say about how the country should be run that they were wrong ...

VERY WRONG!

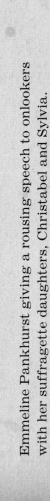

Emmeline Pankhurst giving a rousing speech to onlookers with her suffragette daughters, Christabel and Sylvia.

VOTES FOR WOMEN? NEVER!

Emmeline had a tough time persuading society that VOTES FOR WOMEN was a good idea. The idea shocked and scared some people.

PREPOSTEROUS! Women's brains are FAR too small to handle voting!

GASP! If women get the vote they might stop marrying.

DEEDS NOT WORDS!

Emmeline said the only way to make people take the suffragette message seriously was to use DEEDS NOT WORDS, even if it meant getting into trouble with the police and and sometimes, being sent to prison.

SUFFRAGETTE DEEDS:

Boooo!

Disrupting political speeches

No! I shan't move!

Protesting with banners

Chaining oneself to the railings

SOLDIERS in PETTICOATS

VO GO GIRLS WOMEN

HOORAY! WOMEN GET THE VOTE!

In 1918, the law was finally changed and some women aged over 30 were allowed to vote. It wasn't until 1928, shortly after Emmeline's death, that all women aged over 21 were allowed to vote.

THE SUFFRAGETTES NEED YOU!

If you had been the suffragette to hand out the most copies of the Suffragette newspaper you might have won a new bicycle!

It would have been painted in the suffragette colours – purple, white and green. You could have cycled far and wide recruiting more suffragettes.

Ding-a-ling!

Rosa Parks

Alabama River

MONTGOMERY NEWS

BUS STOP

MONTGOMERY BUS

Rosa Parks stood up for herself and others – by sitting down! Taking the bus home in Montgomery, Alabama, in December 1955, she had no idea that she was about to do something **amazing**.

At the time, strict laws kept white and black people separate. This was called segregation. One law said that if a bus got busy, black people had to give up their seats for white people.

When there were no seats left on the bus, the driver asked Rosa if she was going to give up her seat for a white passenger ...

But Rosa thought to herself, **why should I move?**

ARE YOU GOING TO MOVE?

NO. I am not.

ONE WAY TICKET TO CHANGING THE WORLD

NO SEATS TO BE GIVEN UP

POLICE FILE

ROSA PARKS

Rosa did not budge. She didn't argue or make a fuss, even when she was arrested. She knew she didn't need to shout for her point to be made – that the rules were wrong and unfair.

I'm boycotting the buses.

News of Rosa's arrest spread quickly. Soon other black people decided to stop using buses until the law was changed. Eventually that law, and many other unfair laws were changed.

uh hu. me too!

When Rosa refused to move she took an important step towards making the lives of black and white people equal.

June 1942

Dearest Kitty*,

"I hope I will be able to confide everything to you as I have never been able to confide in anyone ..."

Yours faithfully

Anne Frank

(Aged 13, Amsterdam, Netherlands)

*Anne addressed her diary entries to an imaginary friend called Kitty.

During World War Two, Anne Frank – a girl who dreamed of becoming a writer – had to go into hiding with her family. The war meant life was very unsafe for Jewish people, like the Franks, because they were persecuted by the Nazi party. This meant that Jews were treated unfairly and sent to prison camps, even though they had done nothing wrong.

The Franks hid in a secret annexe – a few concealed rooms in the factory Anne's father ran before the war. They couldn't take many possessions with them, but Anne made sure she took her diary ...

The Frank Family

Anne's father Otto Frank

Anne's mother Edith Frank

Anne's Sister Margot Frank

Anne Frank

"I'm terrified our hiding place will be discovered."

Nobody knew about their hiding place apart from trusted friends who brought supplies. Its entrance was hidden behind a bookshelf.

Anne and Margot on the beach. Happy family life before the war.

Anne poured out all her hopes, frustrations and fears into her diary ...

"Nothing is worse than being caught."

More people who needed to hide came to live with the Franks. Anne found sharing a small space with eight people difficult.

These arguments are driving me crazy.

Food was scarce in the annexe but Anne knew she must put up with it.

The Van Pel Family

Fritz Pfeffer

lettuce

pickled kale

potato

cabbage

anne's family

Anne missed her cat Moortje, who she had to leave behind.

Moortje

"... I still believe in spite of everything, that people are truly good at heart."

Anne's Diary — A Book That Touched the World

After two years everyone living in the annexe was discovered and sent to prison camps. Tragically, only Anne's father survived the war. As a tribute to his amazing daughter, Otto Frank published Anne's Diary. It is a book considered to be one of the most important in history.

Anne never stopped dreaming of a better future. Her hope, talent and bravery has touched the millions of people around the world who have read Anne's diary, *Diary of a Young Girl*.